CW01313498

Nefer Nitty
7130 S Orange Blossom Trail
Suite 112
Orlando, FL 32809

www.nefernitty.com

About the Practice Manual

Congratulations on taking the first steps toward developing or perfecting your Christian mindset as part of the Perfect Peace Project!!

This Practice Manual is designed to help you take control of your thoughts and make them submissive to God's word. Each week, for five days, we will explore a different topic related to a weekly theme. For each day, there will be a Scripture reference related to the topic and a Thought of the Day upon which to focus throughout that day. Following these, you will find a Mindset Exercise.

Each Mindset Exercise is specifically tailored to the day's topic. These Exercises vary with each day and some Exercises you may find are more difficult to accomplish than others. This is to be expected. We are undergoing a serious spiritual journey and it will take fortitude. Don't worry! Jesus has promised to help us gain the victory! (2 Corinthians 5:17; Galatians 5:17).

Some of the Mindset Exercises call for you to watch a film either on YouTube or Amazon Prime Video. If you do not have a subscription, that is okay because the Exercise is never strictly to watch the video nor do they rely on the videos. Think of the videos as enhancements, rather than requirements.

This Project was birthed as a result of me wanting to obtain and hold onto the Perfect Peace as promised in God's word and to show others how to do the same. For accountability and support, it is best completed with a friend, but this is not required. Remember to tune in to the Perfect Peace Podcast as well!
I pray that He will keep you in Perfect Peace. In Jesus' name.

Goals

- To acquire and maintain peace in Christ through trusting in Him.

- To experience the joy of living abundantly, no matter what life's current circumstances may be.

Week 1

God's Love

God's love for me is the foundation of my life. No matter what I go through, I will keep His love for me at the forefront of my mind.

Week 1, Day 1

God Lovingly Provides for My Needs.

Scripture

Today's Date: _________

Psalm 145:15 The eyes of all wait upon thee; and thou givest them their meat in due season.16 Thou openest thine hand, and satisfiest the desire of every living thing.

Philippians 4:19 But my God shall supply all your need according to his riches in glory by Christ Jesus.

Thought of the Day

We may not have everything we want, but we do have everything we need. If we don't recognize this, we need to take time to evaluate this truth in our lives.

Sometimes this may mean that we have to reconsider whether some of the things we think we need are truly necessities.

The society in which you are raised can have a major influence on how you perceive material things in life. What you consider a necessity can be considered by someone else to be a luxury.

Mindset Exercise:

Watch "Happy" (Documentary, 2011) on Amazon Prime or YouTube.

Then:

Focus today on all the things you have. Take time to appreciate what you have.

<u>Make a list of the ways God is providing for your needs.</u>

These can be physical, spiritual, emotional, mental,

the need to love and be loved, etc. Thank God for these things periodically throughout the day.

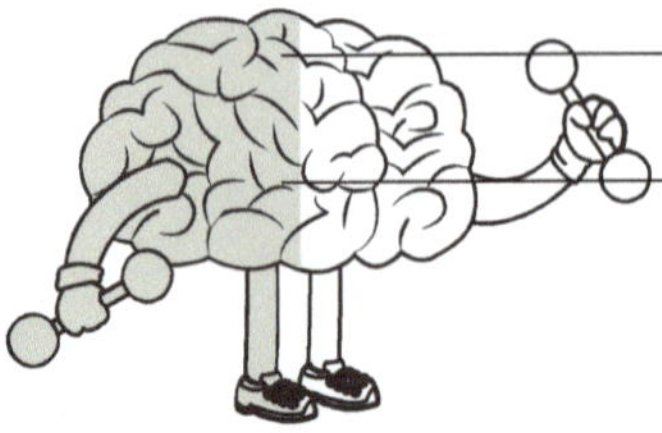

Week 1, Day 2

Even When He Allows Disappointment, it is Out of Love.

Today's Date: ________

Scripture

... cursed is the ground for thy sake; in sorrow shalt thou eat of it all the days of thy life... Genesis 3:17

And we know that all things work together for good to them that love God, to them who are called according to His purpose. Romans 8:28

As many as I love, I rebuke and chasten... Revelation 3:19

Thought of the Day

God never promised to give us a life free from problems. He promised to be with us and see us through our problems. In fact, He uses our problems to develop our characters. We have to keep in mind that when life is hard, that doesn't mean He isn't there or doesn't love us. The Bible actually tells us that it means the exact opposite. It means that He loves us and considers us His children.

Mindset Exercise:

Think about the problems you have experienced in your past or are experiencing currently. Train your mind to see the love of God in those circumstances. Search for God's love in helping you through your problems. Focus on the positive lessons you have learned that have made you more like Christ.

Thank God for bringing you through past trials and thank Him for the fact that He will bring you through current trials.

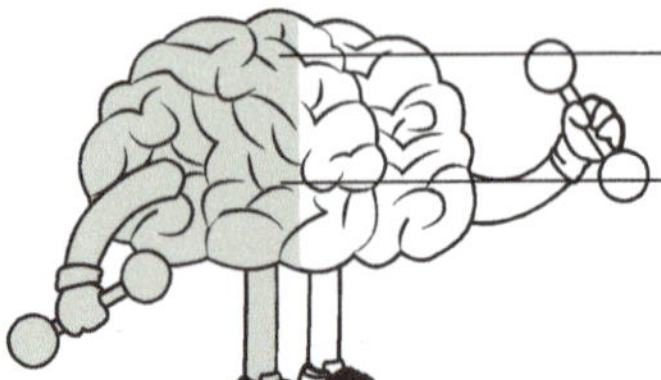

Week 1, Day 3

God Will Never Leave Me.

Scripture

Today's Date: ________

Deuteronomy 31:8 And the Lord, he it is that doth go before thee; he will be with thee, he will not fail thee, neither forsake thee: fear not, neither be dismayed.

Jeremiah 31:3 ... I have loved with with an everlasting love...

Matthew 28:20 ... I am with you always, even unto the end of the world.

Thought of the Day

Separation from the ones you love can cause a great deal of long-lasting pain. When relationships come to an end, it hurts. We often question whether the other person loves us or ever loved us. This is true whether the person is a friend, mate, or family member. Abandonment causes scars.

Your heavenly Father will never leave you. The love He has for you is an everlasting love. He will never abandon you.

Mindset Exercise:

If God is always with you, then you are never alone. You have a life partner. The love that we have been discussing is always with you.

If you sense any resistance to the idea that God's love is always with you, write down why. Ask yourself where these thoughts are coming from. Challenge the negative thoughts to stand up to the Word. Pray and ask God to help you overcome those thoughts.

As you go though your day today, frequently remind yourself that God is with you, that He loves you, and that you are not alone.

Week 1, Day 4

Love is God's Character. God is Love.

Scripture

Today's Date: ________

. . . God is love. 1 John 4:8

Exodus 34:6…"The Lord, the Lord, a God merciful and gracious, slow to anger, and abounding in steadfast love and faithfulness, 7 keeping steadfast love for thousands…

Thought of the Day

Our Father created the world in perfect beauty and even though it is currently corrupted by sin, we can still see His love all around us. He painted the natural scenery with breath-taking colors. Psychologists say colors can affect our emotions. It's interesting to see how the colors having positive effects on us are most present in nature. Animals and insects, wind and water create a beautiful orchestra that also has a positive effect on our emotions. Why would He intentionally do this, if not because He loves us?

Mindset Exercise:

Spend time out in nature today. Absorb the beauty of nature and try to appreciate how God has created this beautiful world for our pleasure. Look up the psychology of nature's most prevalent colors. God's love is evident in the way He designed both our bodies and nature. Nature caters to our physical, emotional and spiritual needs. Thank God for demonstrating His love to us in ways we can't deny. Draw a picture or print and color in a picture of something you find beautiful.

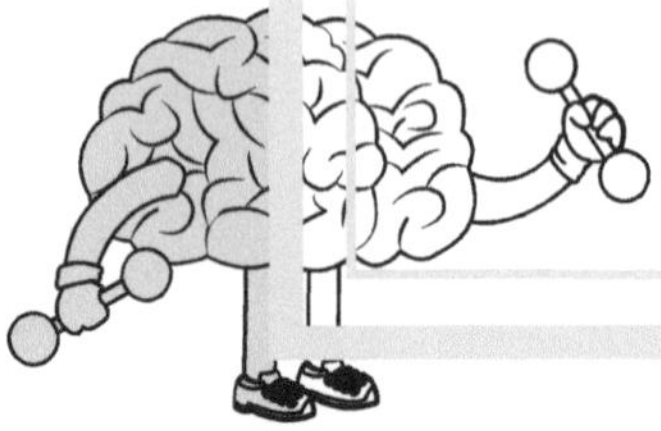

God
is
Love

Week 1, Day 5

God Sacrificed His Son for Me Out of Love.

Scripture

Today's Date: ________

John 3:16 For God so loved the world, that he gave his only Son, that whoever believes in him should not perish but have eternal life.

2 Corinthians 5:19 In Christ God was reconciling the world to himself...

Romans 5:8 ... but God shows his love for us in that while we were still sinners, Christ died for us.

Thought of the Day

We know that God sent His Son to die for our sins, but do we fully appreciate what that means? He sacrificed His only child in order to have a relationship with you. While on earth,Christ's life on earth was filled with doing good. His desire to give us good news, liberty, and sight has not changed (Luke 4:18). Jesus was and still is compassionate, loving, and kind.

This is the love that God has for us.

Mindset Exercise:

Spend time reflecting on the love of God as demonstrated in the life, death, and resurrection of Jesus.

Think about how much someone has to love you to voluntarily die for you so that you can live.

Think about the fact that this same Person knows everything about you and still thinks you are to die for.

Meditate on the fact that God thinks you are worth dying for. That the Creator of all things sacrificed His life for you!

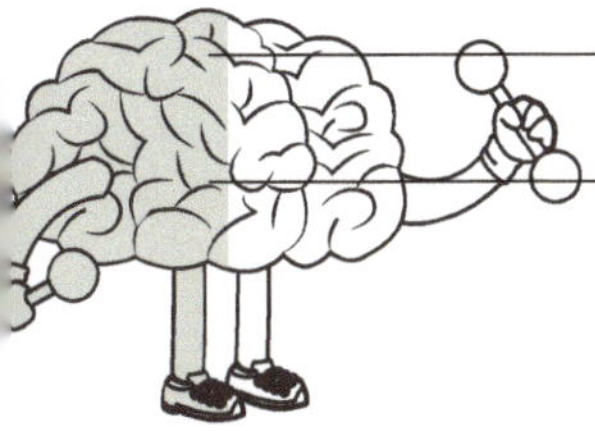

Week 1 Recap - Principles

God's Love

1. God lovingly provides for my needs.
2. Even when He allows disappointment, it is out of love.
3. God will never leave me.
4. Love is God's character. God is Love.
5. God Sacrificed His Son for me out of Love.

Week 1 Recap - Exercises

God's Love

1. Thank God for always providing.
2. Thank God for always seeing you through.
3. Remind yourself that He is always with you.
4. Take time to appreciate God's creation.
5. Remember that God thinks you are to die for!

Week 2

Identity

My identity has to be internal, not external.
I am who God says I am.

Week 2, Day 1

Who am I to God?

Scripture

Today's Date: ________

1 John 3:1 Behold, what manner of love the Father hath bestowed upon us, that we should be called the sons of God...

Zechariah 2:8 8 For thus saith the Lord of hosts; After the glory hath he sent me unto the nations which spoiled you: for he that toucheth you toucheth the apple of His eye.

Thought of the Day

Usually, when we introduce ourselves to someone new, we lead with our name and occupation. Somehow, what we do has become the overarching identifier for who we are. In many cases, telling people what we do for a living can help them know what kind of questions or favors to ask of us and we of them. There's nothing really wrong with that. But the problem with being identified by our occupation is that we internalize this to the extent that we believe we are the job at which we are employed. But jobs and careers are often transient, temporary, changeable.

Week 2, Day 1

Who am I to God?

Today's Date: ________

Thought of the Day(Continued)

Therefore, it is important to anchor our identity in Christ. Who does God say I am? God says that we are His children. 1 John 3:1 says that it is out of love that He calls us His children. This designation is not just a title, but it identifies a depth of a powerful relationship between God and us. You are Gods' child. He goes as far as to call you the apple of His eye.

He says that someone who touches you touches the apple of His eye. You are important to the King of the universe.

Mindset Exercise:

Today, pray that God would fill you with a sense of your importance in His sight. In your journal or a sheet of paper, write out the following verses and ask God to help you internalize their truth. Next to each verse, write out how you are identified in the verse.

1 John 3:1; Zechariah 2:8; Jeremiah 31:3; Zephaniah 3:17; Ephesians 2:10; and 1 Corinthians 6:17.

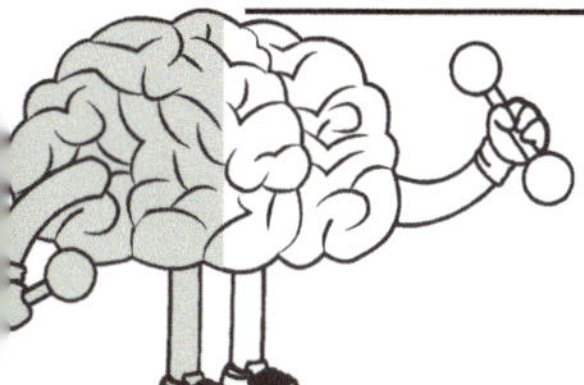

Week 2, Day 2

I am Not Who I Used to Be.

Scripture

Today's Date: ________

2 Corinthians 5:17 Therefore if any man be in Christ, he is a new creature: old things are passed away; behold, all things are become new.

Romans 6:6 Knowing this, that our old man is crucified with him, that the body of sin might be destroyed, that henceforth we should not serve sin.

Psalm 103:12 As far as the east is from the west, so far hath he removed our transgressions from us.

Ephesians 4:24 And that ye put on the new man, which after God is created in righteousness and true holiness.

Thought of the Day

When we think about who we are, we often think about the types of things we do and have done. This is a valid method because the Bible tells us that people are known by their fruits- their character and actions. We have to be very careful, however, not to confuse who we ARE with who we WERE.

Week 2, Day 2

I am Not Who I Used to Be.

Today's Date: ________

Thought of the Day(Continued)

We may have committed shameful sins before committing our lives to Christ. We may have lived a sinful lifestyle, had a devilish mentality, hurt ourselves and other people. But we have been forgiven and cleansed. We can no longer be identified by those sins. In God's eyes, we are no longer associated with them. He has removed them as far as they could go.

Whatever you did in the past is not what God sees when He sees you. That was literally a different life. You are literally a different person now. A new person.

Mindset Exercise:

The Bible and history are full of examples of God changing people's characters and making them into someone almost unrecognizable. The story of the man who wrote the hymn "Amazing Grace" is one such story. Watch "Newton's Grace" on Amazon Prime.

On Day 1 of this week, you wrote out verses and next to them, you wrote how the bible identifies you. Today, write down the identifiers as a list on a very small piece of paper.

Throughout the day, pull out that piece of paper and remind yourself of who a you are in Christ. This way, you are telling yourself and helping yourself believe that you are a new creature in Christ. You don't have to identify with the past. Identify with who God says you are now.

Week 2, Day 3

I am a Servant of the Most High God.

Scripture

Today's Date: ________

2 Corinthians 6:1 We then, as workers together with Him ...

Romans 6:16 Know ye not, that to whom ye yield yourselves servants to obey, his servants ye are to whom ye obey; whether of sin unto death, or of obedience unto righteousness?

Colossians 3:23 And whatsoever ye do, do it heartily, as to the Lord, and not unto men...

Thought of the Day

We talked earlier this week about introducing ourselves by our occupation and how our jobs are tangled up with who we are in the eyes of society and even in our own eyes. Our true occupation as Christians is "Servant of the Lord."We are His children and His servants. We work for Him and He works through us. Employment is defined by Meriam Webster as "use; purpose." So many people struggle with understanding their purpose. The Bible is plain - our purpose is to serve God. That is our function - our use.

Mindset Exercise:

Everything you do today and the rest of the week, do it as if you are working for the Lord. (Colossians 3:23). When you are at work, perform your duties as though your immediate boss was Jesus Himself. As Christians, we often limit the application of these verses to what we think is ministry. But God told us to do all things as though we were doing them for Him. Cleaning the bathroom? Do it for Him. Greeting a customer? Greet them like you're greeting them in His name.

By doing everything like you are at work for Him, you remind yourself of your identity as His servant. And you allow your light to shine so that others can see that same identity in you.

This also helps you raise your thoughts above your current situation. If you are focused on performing your tasks as though they are performed for God Himself, you rise above the common, temporal aspects of what you are doing. Serving Him all day everyday helps to protect you heart from being injured when you are unappreciated at work because you know God appreciates you. It keeps you from feeling like anything you have to do is beneath you because you are doing it for Him.

And the peace of God, which
passeth all understanding,
shall keep your hearts and
minds through Christ Jesus.
Philippians 4:7

Week 2, Day 4

I am God's Representative.

Scripture

Today's Date: ________

John 8:12 Then spake Jesus again unto them, saying, I am the light of the world: he that followeth me shall not walk in darkness, but shall have the light of life.

Matthew 5:14 Ye are the light of the world. A city that is set on an hill cannot be hid.

Exodus 7:1 And the LORD said unto Moses, See, I have made thee a god to Pharaoh: and Aaron thy brother shall be thy prophet.

1 Corinthians 3:16 Know ye not that ye are the temple of God, and that the Spirit of God dwelleth in you?

Thought of the Day

Why does the Bible tell us that Jesus is the Light of the world, and then turn around and tell us that we are the light of the world? Is this a contradiction? No. The Bible explains this phenomenon by letting us know that God lives inside of us. This makes us His representatives. This is why when men see our light, they aren't supposed to glorify us-they are supposed to glorify God.

Week 2, Day 4

I am God's Representative.

Today's Date: ________

Thought of the Day (Continued)

It is His light that they see shining through us. Few people fully grasp what this means. GOD LIVES IN YOU!!

God told Moses that He would make Moses a god unto pharaoh. Moses was God's representative. He was delivering the word of God and the warnings of God. Pharaoh's responses were not responses to Moses but to God Himself. The conversation was between pharaoh and God, with Moses standing as God's representative. This is the relationship God wants to have with all of His children. You are God's representative.

Mindset Exercise:

What does it mean to you to be God's representative? Look back on the other days and the list you made on Day 2. How does it make you feel to hear yourself say these things about yourself? Do you believe them? Do you find them hard to accept? Do they make you happy? Do they bring you comfort? Remember that any thoughts that tell you anything contrary to what the Bible says is a lie. If you feel you are not who the Bible says you are, pray and rebuke those thoughts. Repeat to yourself who God says you are and choose to believe Him rather than believing a lie.

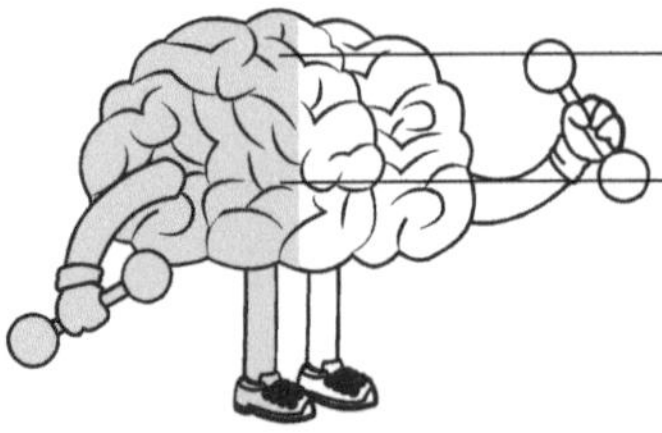

Week 2, Day 5

I am a Unique Member of God's Holy Family.

Scripture

Today's Date: ________

Romans 12:4 For as we have many members in one body, and all members have not the same office: 5 So we, being many, are one body in Christ, and every one members one of another.

Ephesians 2:19 Now therefore ye are no more strangers and foreigners, but fellowcitizens with the saints, and of the household of God;20 And are built upon the foundation of the apostles and prophets, Jesus Christ himself being the chief corner stone;21 In whom all the building fitly framed together groweth unto an holy temple in the Lord:22 In whom ye also are builded together for anhabitation of God through the Spirit.

1 Corinthians 12:12 For as the body is one, and hath many members, and all the members of that one body, being many, are one body: so also is Christ.13 For by one Spirit are we all baptized into one body, whether we be Jews or Gentiles, whether we be bond or free; and have been all made to drink into one Spirit.14 For the body is not one member, but many.

Week 2, Day 5

I am a Unique Member of God's Holy Family.

Today's Date: ________

Thought of the Day

We started this week with our primary identity being children of God. All of God's children are therefore siblings, having the same Father. But even though God has many children, He still thinks of you individually and you are unique in His eyes. The verses above show that each person has their place but collectively, we make up the Body of Christ. The concept of a loving family made up of differing personalities may be easy for some because of the way they were raised by their physical parents. It may be more difficult for others for the same reason.

Wherever you find yourself on this spectrum, remember that the Word is true and every contrary thought is a lie. God has designed a special place for you to fill in this world generally and in His church specifically. The Lord wants us to recognize each other as family.

Mindset Exercise:

Spend time with a member of the holy family today. If you can do this in person, that would be best. If not, then call them. Text only as a last resort. The idea is to genuine spend time with your sibling and talk about your Father. Encourage each other, comfort each other. Bear each other's burdens and rejoice with one another. Enjoy a meal together. Be a family in Christ. Thank Him together for making you siblings.

Week 2 Recap - Principles

Identity

1. Who does God say I am?
2. I am not who I used to be.
3. I am a Servant of the Most High God.
4. I am God's representative.
5. I am a unique member of God's holy family.

Week 2 Recap - Exercises

Identity

1. Internalize who the Bible says you are.
2. You are a new person in Christ.
3. Do everything like you're doing it for Jesus.
4. Repeat to yourself aloud who God says you am.
5. Spend time with your siblings in Christ.

Week 3

Priorities

My priorities reveal my character and my mindset. My priorities need to be grounded in God.

Week 3, Day 1

Where is My Heart?

Scripture

Today's Date: ________

Colossians 3:1 If ye then be risen with Christ, seek those things which are above, where Christ sitteth on
the right hand of God.2 Set your affection on things above, not on things on the earth.

Matthew 6:19 Lay not up for yourselves treasures upon earth, where moth and rust doth corrupt, and where thieves break through and steal:20 But lay up for yourselves treasures in heaven, where neither moth nor rust doth corrupt, and where thieves do not break through nor steal.

Thought of the Day

We are pilgrims in this world, just passing through. We should keep our minds on the ultimate destination of our journey. As Christians, we are aware that we are navigating two planes of existence at the same time- the spiritual and the physical.

Week 3, Day 1

Where is My Heart?

Today's Date: ________

Thought of the Day (Continued)

The saying is often true, "Out of sight, out of mind." We walk in this earth most often preoccupied with our physical world than the spiritual one. The Bible tells us to set our affections on things above. Put our desires on heavenly things. Make spiritual goals. Someone once told me that your priorities are not the things you want to do, they are the things you are already doing. If someone was to ask us to write a list of our priorities and then a second list of the activities that take up most of our time, they would likely be two completely different lists.

Mindset Exercise:

Take some time to reflect and write down 2-3 spiritual/ mental goals you would like to accomplish or work towards this year. These goals should be incorporated into your daily life, so take your time considering what you want to focus on for yourself. It can be a character trait you'd like to develop - like being more giving or forgiving. It could be an evangelistic goal - like drawing souls to Jesus. Any Bible- based principle. No more than 3. This is how we will begin setting our minds on things above.

My Goals

1. ______________________________

2. ______________________________

3. ______________________________

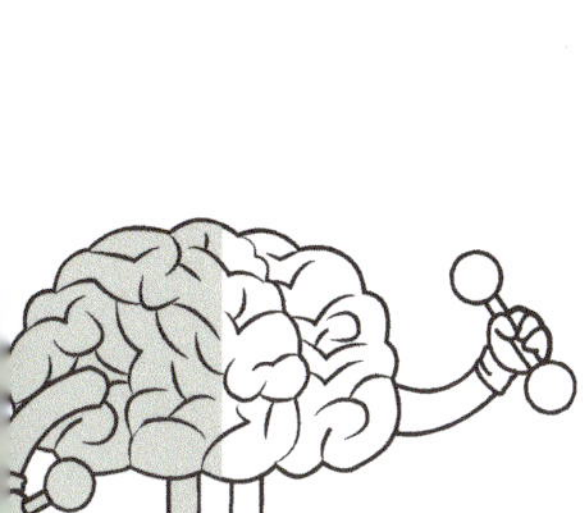

Week 3, Day 2

Seeking God's Kingdom and Righteousness.

Scripture

Today's Date: ________

Matthew 6: 33 But seek ye first the kingdom of God, and his righteousness; and all these things shall be
added unto you.
John 8:29 And he that sent me is with me: the Father hath not left me alone; for I do always those things that please him.

Thought of the Day

What does seeking God first mean to you? It can have two meanings. It can mean to literally let God be the first thing on your mind in the morning and it can mean to make God the first and highest priority in our lives. How can you make God your highest priority? If you are focused on heavenly things, God will be with you and will carry out your desires because your desires will be heaven's desires.

He says to seek His kingdom and His righteousness. We seek His kingdom first by helping to build His kingdom- sharing the gospel with others. You can seek His righteousness by submitting to His will and allowing Him to shape your character.

Mindset Exercise:

Watch"GEORGE MULLER Documentary | A Cloud of Witnesses | FULL" on YouTube

Take your goals from Day 1 of this week and create 2- 3 tasks for each one. Your tasks should be geared towards helping you reach your goal in some small way. For example, if one of your goals is to have a closer prayer walk with the Lord, your tasks can include setting reminders to pray x amount of times a day or writing down a prayer list to encourage you to pray for others. These are just examples.

You will have a list of 4-9 tasks. Next, use your phone's reminder app to schedule reminders throughout the week for you to complete the different tasks for your goals.

Mindset Exercise:

Tasks for my Goals

1. ______________________________
    a. ______________________________
    b. ______________________________
    c. ______________________________

2. ______________________________
    a. ______________________________
    b. ______________________________
    c. ______________________________
3. ______________________________
    a. ______________________________
    b. ______________________________
    c. ______________________________

Peace I leave with
you, my peace I give unto you:
not as the
world giveth, give I unto you.
Let not your heart be troubled,
neither let it be afraid.
John 14:27

Week 3, Day 3

Chase God.

Today's Date: ________

Scripture

1 Timothy 6:9 But those who desire to be rich fall into temptation and a snare, and into many foolish and harmful lusts which drown men in destruction and perdition. 10 For the love of money is a root of all kinds of evil, for which some have strayed from the faith in their greediness, and pierced themselves through with many sorrows. 11 But you, O man of God, flee these things and pursue righteousness, godliness, faith, love, patience, gentleness.

Luke 16:13 No servant can serve two masters: for either he will hate the one, and love the other; or else he will hold to the one, and despise the other. Ye cannot serve God and mammon.

Thought of the Day

The Bible teaches that the pursuit of physical gain can lead our hearts away from God. Self- help books out there typically they tell you that you have to focus on the goal. Usually the goal is financial or business in nature. We gotta chase the bag.

Chase God.

Today's Date: ________

Thought of the Day (Continued)

Even those of us who don't consider ourselves necessarily greedy, still feel like we need to be focused on making money. For some of us, it's a matter of making ends meet. For others, we feel we just need a little more to be comfortable. But the Bible tells us not to set our hearts on money or other earthly valuables.

But it doesn't stop there. God doesn't just tell us what not to do, but He tells us what to do instead. Don't chase the bag. Chase righteousness. Chase godliness and faith. Chase patience and gentleness. What a huge difference this is from what the world tells us to chase.

Mindset Exercise:

What would life look like for you if you didn't have to worry about bills or providing for your basic needs? What would you spend your time doing?

Write about 5 or more sentences about what you think your life would be like. When you are done, read it and recognize the things that are important to you.

Week 3, Day 4

Faith by Experience.

Scripture

Today's Date: ________

Psalm 34:8 O taste and see that the Lord is good: blessed is the man that trusteth in Him.

1 John 5:14 And this is the confidence that we have in him, that, if we ask any thing according to His will, He heareth us:15 And if we know that He hear us, whatsoever we ask, we know that we have the petitions that we desired of Him.

Thought of the Day

The Bible tells us that when we ask God to do something according to His will, He will do it. This does not mean that every prayer that seems good to us will be answered in the way we expect. But He does invite us to taste for ourselves and see that He is good. What we need to keep us grounded in the principles we are practicing is experience. We need experiential faith.

Mindset Exercise:

In the Bible, we see God coming through for people time and time again. We see Him dividing the Red Sea. Sealing shut the mouths of lions. Set people free from prison. Delivered people from death. All in answer to prayer. Today, pray according to His will. Choose something to pray about, not searching for a sign, but seeking an experience. Ask Him for something great. In keeping with the theme for this week, make sure that whatever you pray for is in line with spiritual priorities.

Something that indicates you are seeking first God's kingdom and God's righteousness. When you pray, you must believe what you've already been reading. Believe that He will answer your prayer in the best possible way and that He will withhold no good thing from you (Psalm 84:11). Thank Him while you are still praying. And then look earnestly for the answer to your prayer.

Mindset Exercise:

Week 3, Day 5

Biblical Meditation

Scripture

Today's Date: ________

Joshua 1:8 This book of the law shall not depart out of thy mouth; but thou shalt meditate therein day and night, that thou mayest observe to do according to all that is written therein: for then thou shalt make thy way prosperous, and then thou shalt have good success.

Psalm 19:14 Let the words of my mouth, and the meditation of my heart, be acceptable in thy sight, O Lord, my strength, and my redeemer.

Psalm 1:1 Blessed is the man that walketh not in the counsel of the ungodly, nor standeth in the way of sinners, nor sitteth in the seat of the scornful. 2 But his delight is in the law of the Lord; and in his law doth he meditate day and night. 3 And he shall be like a tree planted by the rivers of water, that bringeth forth his fruit in his season; his leaf also shall not wither; and whatsoever he doeth shall prosper.

Week 3, Day 5

Biblical Meditation

Today's Date: ________

Thought of the Day

God asks us to meditate on His word. This simply means to think about it. Dissect it mentally. Memorize it and apply it to your life. When we are young and we fall in love or find someone we are interested in, we think of them all day long - even when we are busy doing other things. Girls daydream and write the name of their love interest in their notebooks. This is the way we should be thinking about God and the principles He has set out for us to live by.

Mindset Exercise:

Make a list of the principles we have gone over up to now, in your own words. Make each principle short. You will repeat these principles to yourself daily. As we repeat them, they will become ingrained in our minds. Repeat the principles or scriptures associated with them. Remember that the Peace Project is one that works on our minds. We are training our minds to think heavenly thoughts so that we can have peace.

Checkpoint

Without looking back at the previous days, write down what principles you can remember from each of the topics we have covered so far.

God's Love

Identity

Priorities

Week 3 Recap Principles

Priorities

1. Where is my heart?
2. Seek God's kingdom and righteousness.
3. Chase God.
4. Faith by experience.
5. Biblical meditation.

Week 3 Recap - Exercises

Priorities

1. Set my mind on things above by setting spiritual goals.
2. Take time daily to complete tasks that will help me reach my goals.
3. Recognize the things that are important to me.
4. Make a prayer request to God to build faith.
5. Keep the practice principles in mind.

Week 4

Mindset Habits

Having established certain principles, I will now focus on the way I think.

Week 4, Day 1

I Have the Power to Control My Mind.

Scripture

Today's Date: ________

Proverbs 4:23 Keep thy heart with all diligence; for out of it are the issues of life.

2 Corinthians 10:4 (For the weapons of our warfare are not carnal, but mighty through God to the pulling down of strong holds;)5 Casting down imaginations, and every high thing that exalteth itself against the knowledge of God, and bringing into captivity every thought to the obedience of Christ

Thought of the Day

In the Bible, the words heart and mind are generally interchangeable. The Bible tells us to "keep" our hearts. The Good News Translation reads, "Be careful how you think; your life is shaped by your thoughts." You have the power to guard your thoughts and the way you think. Every thought can be taken captive and made subject to Jesus. God tells us to control our thoughts, so we can and we should.

Mindset Exercise:

Observe yourself and your thoughts today. Study the way you think about things. Get to know yourself in this way. Most people are on auto-pilot, and do not reflect on their own behavior. How can you take control of your thoughts if you are not aware of your thought patterns?

Week 4, Day 2

Choose Good Thoughts

Scripture

Today's Date: ________

Proverbs 23:7 As a man thinketh in his heart, so is he.

Philippians 4:8 ...whatsoever things are true, whatsoever things are honest, whatsoever things are just, whatsoever things are pure, whatsoever things are lovely, whatsoever things are of good report; if there be any virtue, and if there be any praise, think on these things.

Thought of the Day

We have the power to control our thoughts. Shouldn't we choose to have good thoughts? If you want to have peaceful and pure thoughts, you have to focus on peaceful and pure things. The Bible says that your thoughts make you who you are. You can change your mindset and in turn, this will change your character.

Mindset Exercise:

Make an intentional effort today to find the beauty in life around you. If you find yourself feeling down, redirect your thoughts to things you are grateful for, the attributes of God's character, or happy memory you have.

Life is Beautiful!

Week 4, Day 3

Reject Evil Influences

Scripture

Today's Date: ________

Psalm 101:3 I will set no wicked thing before mine eyes: I hate the work of them that turn aside; it shall not cleave to me.

Luke 11:34 The light of the body is the eye: therefore when thine eye is single, thy whole body also is full of light; but when thine eye is evil, thy body also is full of darkness.

Psalm 1:1 Blessed is the man that walketh not in the counsel of the ungodly, nor standeth in the way of sinners, nor sitteth in the seat of the scornful.

James 4:7 Submit yourselves therefore to God. Resist the devil, and he will flee from you.

Thought of the Day

Resisting evil influences sounds like a difficult task. Because most of the time, it is. We learned yesterday that we should choose to the center our thoughts on good things. Resisting evil influences is just a part of that effort. Science is pretty clear that despite how strong we think we may be to withstand influence, we are all subject to it.

Reject Evil Influences

Today's Date: ________

Thought of the Day (Continued)

The Bible encourages us to not set wicked things before our eyes. Jesus told us that if our eyes cause us to sin, we should (metaphorically) pluck them out. (Matthew 18:9). He also told us that to look at one another lustfully is the same as committing adultery. (Matthew 5:28; 2 Peter 2:14). As mentioned before, the mind and the heart are interchangeable- they mean the same thing.

We can see therefore that there is a direct relationship between the things we watch, the people we associate with (Psalm 1:1, for example), and the thoughts we have. We must recognize this as fact. Our opinions about our ability to resist the evil influence of ungodly things while we indulge in them needs to be checked by the Word of God.

The promise is that if we submit to God and resist the devil, the devil will flee from us. Let's get rid of the evil practices and influences that are negatively affecting our thoughts.

Mindset Exercise:

Watch Battlefield Hollywood on YouTube.

Try and recognize any evil influences you are allowing in your life. Try to resist or avoid them. If they are ungodly people, change the nature of the relationship so that you are making about their salvation, rather than simply enjoying their company. You may have to end the relationship altogether. If it is ungodly entertainment, turn it off and ask God for the strength to resist watching it. Ask Him to purify your desires so that you won't want to watch it anymore. Make a covenant with your eyes, ears, and heart.

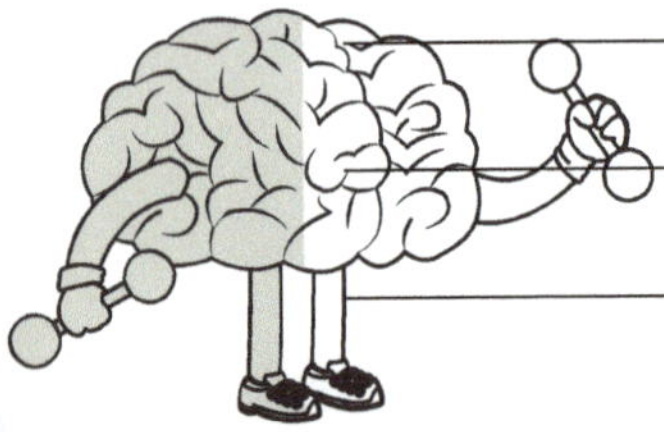

Week 4, Day 4

It Takes Exercise

Scripture

Today's Date: ________

Proverbs 4:8 But the path of the just is as the shining light, that shineth more and more unto the perfect day.

2 Peter 3:18 But grow in grace, and in the knowledge of our Lord and Saviour Jesus Christ. To him be glory both now and for ever. Amen.

1 Corinthians 9:25 And every man that striveth for the mastery is temperate in all things. Now they do it to obtain a corruptible crown; but we an incorruptible.

Luke 9:23And he said to them all, If any man will come after me, let him deny himself, and take up his cross daily, and follow me.

Thought of the Day

The principles and exercises we have been applying the past four weeks are difficult. It takes time to make them a habit. Be encouraged, however, that God is giving you strength to grow in grace. Everyone knows exercises dormant muscles hurts at first. You just have to humbly take up your cross and follow Him. Do not be discouraged if you feel as though you don't have Perfect Peace yet. It is a process. Aand it is a promise. You WILL receive it if you live by the Word.

Mindset Exercise:

Read the verses from today and select your favorite one to memorize. Then, go back through each week's recap and write down the your favorite principles and exercises that you would like to continue practicing, even though this portion of the project has been completed.

Week 4, Day 5

Rest in His Promises

Scripture

Today's Date: ________

John 16:33 These things I have spoken unto you, that in me ye might have peace. In the world ye shall have tribulation: but be of good cheer; I have overcome the world.

Psalm 46:10 Be still, and know that I am God ...

Number 6:24 The Lord bless thee, and keep thee:25 The Lord make his face shine upon thee, and be gracious unto thee:26 The Lord lift up his countenance upon thee, and give thee peace.

John 14:27 27 Peace I leave with you, my peace I give unto you: not as the world giveth, give I unto you. Let not your heart be troubled, neither let it be afraid.

Philippians 4:6 Be careful for nothing; but in every thing by prayer and supplication with thanksgiving let your requests be made known unto God.7 And the peace of God, which passeth all understanding, shall keep your hearts and minds through Christ Jesus.

2 Thessalonians 3:16 Now the Lord of peace himself give you peace always by all means. The Lord be with you all.

Week 4, Day 5

Rest in His Promises

Today's Date: ________

Thought of the Day

You have labored for four weeks, working on your mindset in order to obtain Perfect Peace. You should be proud of yourself for sticking with it! You may not yet be convinced that there have been changes in your mindset, but I believe that you have, even if you haven't recognized it yet.

If you have done and continue to do your part, you can safely rest in the promises of God, knowing that He is the one who puts the desire in us to do good and gives us the power to do it. (Philippians 2:13)

Mindset Exercise:

Rest in His Promises

Week 4 Recap - Principles

Mindset Habits

1. I have the power to control my thoughts.
2. Choose good thoughts.
3. Reject evil influences.
4. It takes exercise.
5. Rest in His Promises.

Week 4 Recap - Exercises

Mindset Habits

1. Reflect on your own thought patterns.
2. Choose to focus on the good in life.
3. Get rid of evil influences under your control.
4. Reflect on the principles you've learned.
5. Rest in His promises.

CPSIA information can be obtained
at www.ICGtesting.com
Printed in the USA
LVHW071533280920
667301LV00021B/1827

9798617440500